CW01099676

Beau Brummie's A to Z of Football

Hi football fans, I'm Beau Brummie.
Welcome to my A to Z of Football.
I hope you enjoy learning about the
game and the best team in the world.
See you at the match,

love,

Concept and words: Andy Favell
Illustration and design: Lance Bell

First Edition, published in July 2007 in hardback and paperback
by Mascot Publishing (UK), PO Box 58810, London SE15 3WU.
Email: mascot@pobox.com; web: www.mascotpublishing.co.uk

Hardback edition – ISBN 978-0-9554426-1-2
Paperback edition – ISBN 978-0-9554426-2-9

Printed in Malta

Beau Brummie

is a very lucky dog

Beau Brummie plays football
for the Birmingham City team.
**"The greatest football team
the world has ever seen!"**

That is Beau holding the ball.
Why don't you say **"Hello"**?
He is between Gary and Goalie,
and the Manager ends the row.

Gary   Beau   Goalie   The Manager

Aa

is for away

Every other match
Birmingham City play away.
The Blues are off to London
to play the Bears today.

Beau Brummie is very excited –
he is going to see Big Ben.
What other sights will the Blues see
on the way to the Bears' den?

Bb

is for Bluenose

The Blues are playing at home
and all the Bluenose fans are here.
It helps the team to play their best
when the loyal fans sing and cheer.

Let's sing along with the Bluenoses:
"We are on our way!
We are on our way!
The Blues are on their way!"

Cc

is for captain

Today Beau is team captain.
It makes him very proud
to lead out Birmingham City
in front of the cheering crowd.

Can you see the captain's armband?
On the pitch, Beau is the boss.
"Mark that striker," he tells Gary,
"and do not let him cross!"

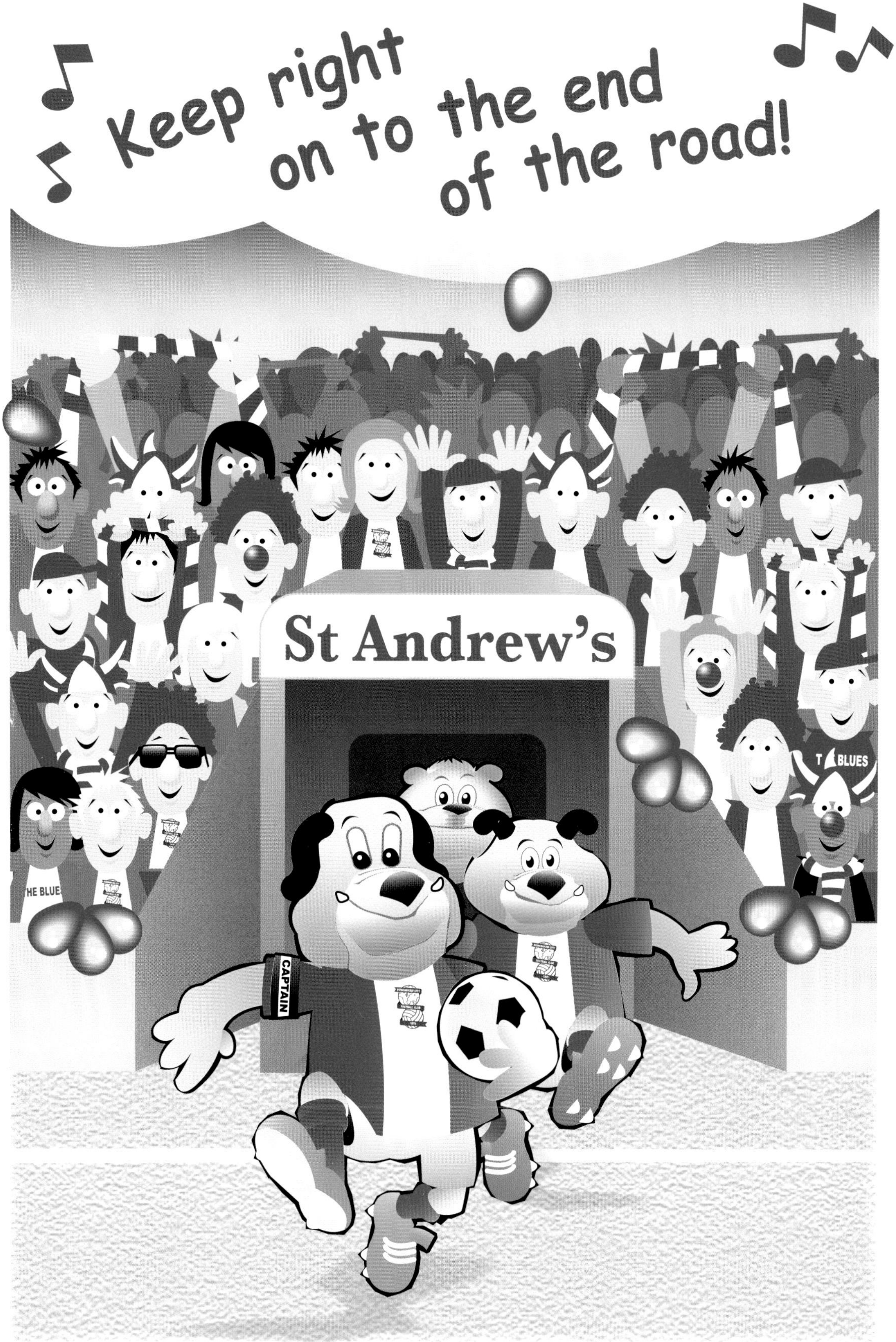
Keep right on to the end of the road!
St Andrew's
CAPTAIN

Dd

is for defender

The Badgers run up the pitch,
the Blues' goal is under attack.
Now the City players must defend
to stop the Badgers in their tracks.

Gary tackles the Badgers' striker
and steals the ball away.
Now the Birmingham goal is safe.
"Well played!" He is on form today.

Ee

is for eleven

How many Blues are in the team?
Let's count the players.
The goalkeeper guards the goal,
helped by the four defenders.

Four Blues play in midfield:
two in the centre, two wings out wide.
Finally add two strikers up front,
making eleven players in the side.

Ff

is for foul

In football, just as in life,
everyone must obey the rules.
Breaking the rules is called a foul –
fouls are only committed by fools.

Handle the ball, push, pull or trip
and any other dirty trick:
beep! goes the referee's whistle
and the other team has a free kick.

Gg

is for goal

Football is all about scoring goals –
getting the ball in the net is the aim.
If they score more than the Crocodiles,
Birmingham City will win the game.

Look at that great pass from Gary.
Beau is going to take a shot, I bet.
Will the ball go past the goalkeeper
and score a goal in the Crocs' net?

 "Come on Beau! Come on Beau!"

Hh

is for header

Gary is dribbling down the wing,
he turns, ready to cross the ball.
The striker runs towards the goal.
"Over here on my head!" Beau calls.

Gary kicks the ball across the goal,
picking out Beau with great skill.
Beau jumps and heads the ball.
The Blues are winning two goals to nil.

"There's only one Beau Brummie!"

Ii

is for injury

Oh dear! What's happened here?
Ouch! Beau falls and hurts his knee.
The doctor says he cannot play on
because he must rest his injury.

The stretcher is brought over
and poor Beau is lifted on.
A reserve player will replace him –
this is called a substitution.

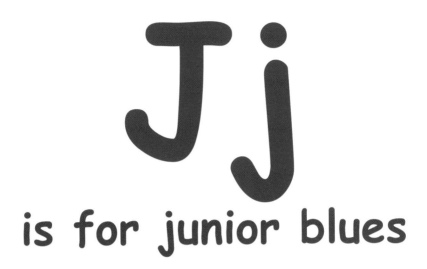

is for junior blues

This is Beau's little brother Jasper.
He is mad about football too.
On Saturdays he watches the match
like every true junior blue.

After Jasper has done his homework,
the brothers practise in the yard.
If Jasper is going to play for the Blues,
he will have to work very hard.

Kk

is for kit

The day before a big match,
Beau prepares all his kit.
He is very proud to play
in the Birmingham City strip.

He lays out his socks and shorts
and irons his blue and white shirt.
Then he checks his football boots
and polishes away any dirt.

is for lose

The whistle has blown – **beep!**
Oh no! The Weasels have won.
The Weasels scored two goals,
while the Blues have only one.

The whole team tried their best
and no player is to blame.
This week they will train hard,
so they win their next game.

is for manager

Who is the cleverest of all the Blues?
The Manager, haven't you heard?
The lads know he is a football expert
and listen carefully to every word.

The Manager picks the team,
keeping some players in reserve.
He plans the next game carefully
and helps the lads keep their nerve.

is for national team

To play for Birmingham City
fills the Blues with pride.
But all players dream of the day
they play for their national side.

For each and every footballer,
it is an honour to be called up.
The ultimate dream is to play
for their country in the World Cup.

Oo

is for own goal

Beau kicks the ball in the Blues' net.
Oops! Giving away a goal is bad.
Now Birmingham City are losing
and the Manager looks very mad.

Poor Beau! Scoring an own goal
is such an unlucky thing to do.
The Manager is shouting at Beau:
"Try scoring at the other end too!"

Aa Bb Cc Dd Ee Ff Gg Hh Ii Jj Kk Ll Mm

Pp

is for penalty kick

Beau is in the penalty area,
from here he is bound to score.
Then the cat trips him up – **oh no!**
Beau lands flat on the floor.

The referee blows his whistle – **beep!**
It's a penalty, everyone stand back.
Beau puts the ball on the penalty spot,
then kicks it in the net with a **whack!**

"Hooray for Beau. It's a GOAL!"

Nn Oo **Pp** Qq Rr Ss Tt Uu Vv Ww Xx Yy Zz

Aa Bb Cc Dd Ee Ff Gg Hh Ii Jj Kk Ll Mm

is for queue

Half an hour before a big game
the queues start to form.
Blue and white hats and scarves
keep the City fans nice and warm.

Streaming through the turnstiles
are Bluenoses of every sort.
All here to boost the players
with their passionate support.

Nn Oo Pp **Qq** Rr Ss Tt Uu Vv Ww Xx Yy Zz

Rr

is for referee

Beep! Who is that in black
blowing the whistle?
That is the referee –
the policeman of football.

In his book, the ref writes
the naughty monkey's name.
"Do not misbehave again
or you'll be out of the game!"

Ss

is for St Andrew's

St Andrew's is the home
of the Birmingham City team.
To play at this ground
is every Junior Blue's dream.

For more than 100 years
City have played football here.
"Come on you Blues!"
the Bluenose fans loudly cheer.

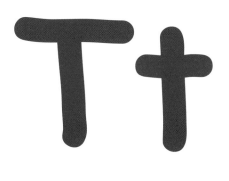

is for training

At 10 o'clock each morning,
the players start their training.
They do exercises and run races,
even when it is cold or raining.

After eating a healthy lunch,
the Blues work on ball control.
Then the strikers practise passing
and shooting balls at the goal.

Uu

is for up

Birmingham City win their game,
while the Stripes and Rabbits lose.
Now the Blues have overtaken
both teams – **what great news!**

The City fans are very excited
and sing the praises of Beau's crew.
The Bluenoses jump to their feet:
"Stand up, if you love the Blues!"

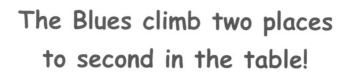

Vv

is for veteran

This is Beau's grandpa Alfie.
He was a famous Blue years ago.
He thinks he is a football expert,
the grumpy old so-and-so.

"These lads are soft," he mutters,
"come on boys, get stuck in!"
But secretly Alfie is proud of Beau,
cheering loudly when the Blues win.

Ww

is for win

In the last minute of the game,
Beau shoots and scores.
The Rabbits have two goals,
but the Blues win with four.

The fans stand and applaud
the team's excellent display.
The St Andrew's faithful sing:
"The Blues are on their way!"

marks the spot

Let's play a game of spot the ball.
Are you ready to mark the spot?
Gary took a strike at the goal –
did the goalkeeper stop his shot?

The football is missing –
where do you think it should be?
Beau thinks the ball is in the net.
He asks: **"Do you agree?"**

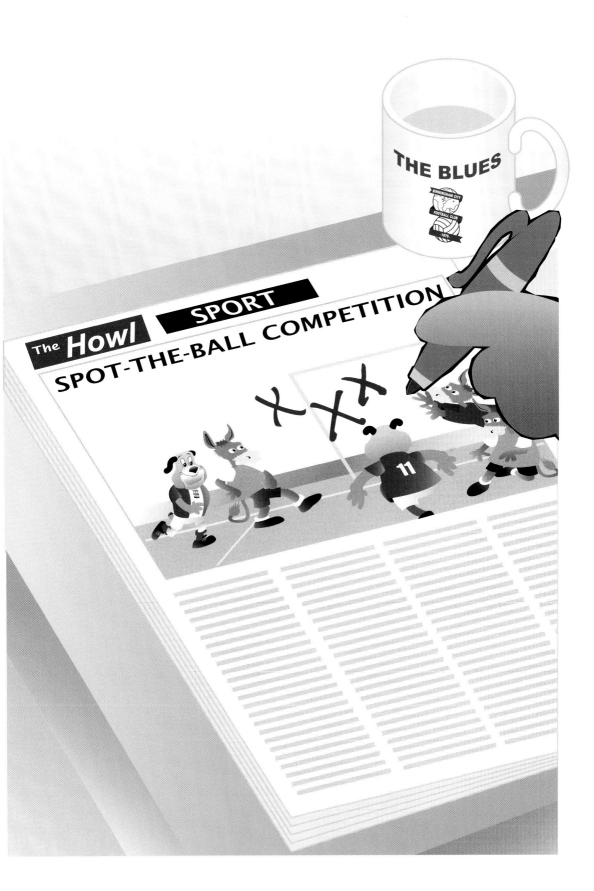

is for you

Why do Beau and the Blues
try their best every game?
They train hard every day –
do they do it just for the fame?

"**Whether we win or lose,**" says Beau,
"**the Bluenose fans stay true.**
Our supporters are our twelfth man:
we couldn't do it without you!"

Zz

is for ZZZZ

The Blues are heading home,
City were on top form today.
The happy lads are singing
on the way up the motorway.

Beau's eyes become heavy.
He is ready for a snooze.
He drifts off, while humming
the tune to **"Singing the Blues!"**

Are you the biggest Blues supporter? Then you will be sure to join THE official Birmingham City fan club for young Bluenoses: Beau's Buddies.

Beau's Buddies is the BCFC young supporters' club for boys and girls aged 0 to 8 years old. It's fun-packed, full of competitions and events, and keeps you up-to-date on all the latest Blues news.

Every member of Beau's Buddies will receive:

- Beau's Buddies welcome pack
- Membership card
- Birthday card
- Exclusive invites to all Beau's Buddies events throughout the season, including the Christmas Party and the End of Season Party!
- Exclusive offers at the club shop throughout the season
- Exclusive competitions to win prizes *that money can't buy*
- Free entry to BCFC reserve games
- Newsletters
- And much more

For more information about Beau's Buddies and for an application form, call 0844 557 1411.